# Words
# are not
# things

D1341039

# Words are not things

## Jack
Gardner

## foulsham
London • New York • Toronto • Sydney

# foulsham

The Publishing House, Bennetts Close,
Cippenham, Slough, Berkshire, SL1 5AP,
England

ISBN-13: 978-0-572-03040-7
ISBN-10: 0-572-03040-1

A CIP record of this book is available from the British Library.

Printed in Great Britain by St Edmundsbury Press Ltd, Bury St Edmunds
Designed by Room 7 Limited Advertising and Design. www.room7.uk.com

for
Rachel

Although I started writing this book whilst in Japan and have spent a great deal of time reading about Zen philosophy and Japanese culture, I cannot tell you what Zen is. If you want to know more about it, you must make that journey for yourself, as I did. I cannot even tell you where to begin as that in itself is part of the journey.

However, I have used one Zen technique for helping students seeking enlightenment. The unusual typography is used deliberately to interrupt habitual and predictable actions or thought processes. The text display prevents easy reading patterns and disrupts the reader's comprehension of each aphorism, hopefully causing deeper thought and consideration.

And on the subject of thought, the purpose of this book is just that: to provoke thought. It is a fact that you can improve your brainpower by exercising your thought processes. Use this book to do it. Take a page at a time, don't rush, be calm and contemplate the meaning. There are no definitive answers; everyone will have their own interpretation of each aphorism depending on where they are in their lives.

# Be there before you leave here.

Listen for the creak of the bow not

the

rush of the arrow

# Happiness is
# not
# just the
absence of unhappiness

# Fifty years ago they said,

# 'in fifty years' time...'

When you learn a

# fact

## you lose
### an ignorance

# Too many simples become complicated

# Think

before you say to

## someone,

# 'look'

# If nothing

# else

is available,

clutch at straws

Your mouth is
the tap,
your words
are the
water

You must have a rough

idea

of the time to believe

a clock

# Words are not thoughts

A dog can only ever

# be
a dog

# An apology should always

include the offence

Autumn leaves are
# beautiful

# but dead

If, in the future, a

# snake

is going to

# bite you,

it is unavoidable

# You
## are already
# there

Guns are made
in one factory,

bullets
in another

If there is a part of

# your

life you don't
want, don't live it

# The perfect
## temperature is never
# noticed

# The
# best plate will
# taste of nothing

You will never know

your inner self

until
you

can see through your outer self

# If you

wait long enough,

## suddenly

### nothing will

# happen

# One step

## is a complete journey

A wrongly spelt word

# does not

change its meaning in a

# sentance

# You
## own your
# stress

# Make sure your enemies think more about you than you do about them

# Your mind is always made
# up

# Above all
# your

skills and weapons,

your enemy fears

your courage most

Never be angry with
something that
**can't get**
angry with you

# Advice will never hurt the giver

# The longer

interesting journey

is always shorter

## than the

shorter boring one

Fear of death is not the same

# as the

love of life

Do not ask questions until

# you

have trained yourself

not to know the

# answers

# The

deer have their paths
through
the forest,
we have ours

Name your target after the arrow has landed

Triumphs separate

disappointments, just

as

disappointments separate triumphs

# Unhappiness

is sought out with

enthusiasm that makes

it appear desirable

# We

think we are being

interesting to others when

we are being interesting to

## ourselves

# Once we demand a proof, it is no longer a faith

When there is only
one possible
action,
the only decision is

when

A glimpse in a mirror
is always
more
revealing than a stare

We choose

the

morality that suits our

ambitions

# Straight
## answers can
only be given to straight
## questions

# Look
inward for the
most distant
### view

You cannot choose

# what

you remember

If you do nothing,
everything is

# easy

# Do not mistake information

# for knowledge

# Anger is seen as a weapon by the coward

We need
surprisingly
little to remain alive
but so
much more to live

# How do you put your thoughts in order?

# There is never

# just

one motive for any action

Camouflage grabs attention

# when
# out
# of context

# Money

is a shared illusion

# Change is always ahead of

# us,

## never behind

# Always try

to be there before you leave here

# Your
## memory
is everything you
have not forgotten

# Gibberish
# IS

creativity that nobody else understands

# People
# will
## willingly
mistake anything for proof

# Desire is as abstract

# as
# smoke

The past has

# been

through your eyes

Boring is the right thought at the wrong time

Being determined does **not** require a task

# Loneliness is
# never
## cured by people

The dead will give

# you

better advice

# than

the living

# Feelings

# do

## not answer when called

# People listen to voices

# not

# words

Teaching does not necessarily

# lead to
# learning

# You move around your shadow

# When you say
# I believe,

do you mean, I want you
to believe, I believe?

# Forever takes time

# React

to what you feel

# not

to what you know

# If you fear everything, you never see danger

# Two
## same notes
### do not make a
# harmony

# No one will
# lie
## to you more than your
# imagination

Knowing what wisdom

# is is

the hardest piece of

wisdom to acquire

A drowned horse

hasn't

necessarily drunk

# Most good luck goes unnoticed;

bad luck never does

# From a list

of outcomes, failure is

sometimes the wisest choice

A person who stands perfectly still **is** always noticed

Never offer advice

# just

to appear
concerned

If you have a faith in something that cannot be proved, you must believe in everyone

# else's
# faiths

Coincidences happen **all the time,** but go unnoticed

When something is

so familiar you can

do it with your eyes

# shut,
# don't

# Success must be used immediately

# Value is not

## determined by price

# but
## by need

A comment that starts

# with

the words 'I think',
usually means the opposite

What you decide is
# perfect
is entirely your
# decision

# Bite size

knowledge is not
always easy to swallow

The more knots in
a rope,
the
shorter it gets

Preparation is an end in

# itself

# When love feels wrong it probably is

# Only you
# can
turn information into
# knowledge

# Feeling secure is a warning

If you want to remember what you were thinking, think about what you

# were doing

In a half you
will always
see
the whole

Where utility ends

# and

decoration begins is

# perfection

# The

most valuable possession is good

# luck

The wisest words can

# be the

worst advice

# Silence
## is the loudest
# noise

# Wisdom

is always obvious

Treat the idiot like a genius and the genius like an

# idiot

and you will never

# be wrong

If you stand on
your possessions
you will see
further;
if you carry them
they will crush you

# If it

has gone and you are alive, you didn't need it

Question the question

# before

# asking it

# Meditation is contemplation without a subject

# Time
# is not
# joined up

# The world in your head is not round

# If you

desire tomorrow,

# you

throw away today

If the food is bad,
look first to
the
recipe, not the cook

# Desire
# the
# inevitable

Dreaming is
what your
mind does when
you
are away

# Crisis is *a* solution

The object of
your desire is

# not

an object

# No answer is an answer

A sword made of gold
is the most valuable

# but

useless

for fighting

# All my
time alone
I spend with
# you

# Experience
## will tell you
### if you need more
# of it

# Where words end is...

It was Robert who first took me to temple thirty
two in Mitagawa and stood with me in the
snowy, freezing, blue dusk, where this all began.

# arcanum arcanorum